Field Trips and Fund-Raisers

Introducing Fractions

Catherine Twomey Fosnot

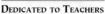

DEDICATED TO TEACHERS

*first*hand
An imprint of Heinemann
361 Hanover Street
Portsmouth, NH 03801–3912
firsthand.heinemann.com

Offices and agents throughout the world

ISBN 13: 978-0-325-01023-6
ISBN 10: 0-325-01023-4

Harcourt School Publishers
6277 Sea Harbor Drive
Orlando, FL 32887–6777
www.harcourtschool.com

ISBN 13: 978-0-15-360575-8
ISBN 10: 0-15-360575-8

The development of a portion of the material described within was supported in part
by the National Science Foundation under Grant No. 9911841. Any opinions, findings,
and conclusions or recommendations expressed in these materials are those of the
authors and do not necessarily reflect the views of the National Science Foundation.

Library of Congress Cataloging-in-Publication Data
CIP data is on file with the Library of Congress

Printed in the United States of America on acid-free paper

11 10   ML   3 4 5 6

Acknowledgements

Photography

Herbert Seignoret
Mathematics in the City, City College of New York

Illustrator

Meryl Treatner

Schools featured in photographs

The Muscota New School/PS 314 (an empowerment school in Region 10), New York, NY
Independence School/PS 234 (Region 9), New York, NY
Fort River Elementary School, Amherst, MA

Contents

Unit Overview

The focus of this unit is the development of fractions. It begins with the story of a class field trip. The class split into four groups and each group was given submarine sandwiches to share for lunch. Upon returning from their trip, the students quarreled over whether some received more to eat than others.

Note: This unit begins with the fair sharing of submarine sandwiches on a field trip. This context was field-tested by the Freudenthal Institute and the University of Wisconsin, under the direction of Thomas Romberg and Jan de Lange, in preparation for the writing of *Mathematics in Context: Some of the Parts* (van Galen, Wijers, Burrill, and Spence 1997) and it has been researched and written about extensively as it is used in this unit by Fosnot and Dolk (2002).

This story context sets the stage for a series of investigations in this unit. First, students investigate whether the situation in the story was fair—was the quarreling justified?—thereby exploring the connection between division

The Landscape of Learning

BIG IDEAS

- Fractions are relations—the size or amount of the whole matters
- Fractions may represent division with a quotient less than one
- With unit fractions, the greater the denominator, the smaller the piece is
- Pieces don't have to be congruent to be equivalent
- For equivalence, the ratio must be kept constant

STRATEGIES

- Using landmark unit fractions or using common fractions
- Using decimal and/or percentage equivalents
- Using a ratio table as a tool to make equivalent fractions
- Using multiplication and division to make equivalent fractions
- Using a common whole to compare fractions

MODELS

- Fair sharing
- Ratio table
- Measurement
- Fraction bars
- Double open number line

and fractions, as well as ways to compare fractional amounts. As the unit progresses, students explore other cases to determine fair sharing and then make a ratio table to ensure fair sharing during their future field trips. They also design a 60k bike course for a fund-raiser, a context that introduces a bar model for fractions and provides students with another opportunity to explore equivalent fractions.

Several minilessons for division of whole numbers using simplified equivalents are also included in the unit. These are structured using strings of related problems as a way to more explicitly guide learners toward computational fluency with whole-number division and to build a connection to equivalent fractions.

Note: The context for this unit assumes that your students have had prior experience with arrays for multiplication and division, as well as partitive and quotative division with whole numbers. If this is not the case, you might find it helpful to first use the units *The Teachers' Lounge* and *Minilessons Throughout the Year: Multiplication and Division.*

The Mathematical Landscape

Have you ever watched students trying to fold a strip of paper into thirds? Because this is so difficult to do, they often make three equal pieces first and then snip off the sliver of the strip that remains and declare they have made thirds! Of course they have changed the whole, so they do not have 1/3 of the original strip, just three congruent pieces with part of the strip thrown away! Constructing the idea that fractions are relations and thus the size or the amount of the whole matters is an important big idea underlying an understanding of fractions. The conception that removing a small piece doesn't matter results from fractions being taught as a shading activity of part-whole relations divorced from division. Research by Leen Streefland (1991) of the Freudenthal Institute in the Netherlands has shown that learners would do better if they started exploring fractions in more realistic fair-sharing contexts, such as one candy bar shared among three people. No child is willing to discard a piece in this context!

This unit is designed to encourage the development of some of the big ideas underlying fractions:

❖ *fractions are relations—the size or amount of the whole matters*

❖ *fractions may represent division (both partitive and quotative forms) with a quotient less than one*

❖ *with unit fractions, the greater the denominator, the smaller the piece is*

❖ *pieces don't have to be congruent to be equivalent*

❖ *for equivalence, the ratio must be kept constant*

❖ Fractions are relations—the size or amount of the whole matters

Fractions are relations: a ratio of part to whole (3 parts out of 4) or a rate (3 sandwiches for 4 people). Fractions can also be operators. For example, $\frac{3}{5}$ could actually be more than $\frac{4}{5}$, if we are talking about $\frac{3}{5}$ *of* 15 versus $\frac{4}{5}$ *of* 10! Constructing the idea that fractions are relations and that the size or amount of the whole matters is a critical step in understanding fractions.

❖ Fractions may represent division (both partitive and quotative forms) with a quotient less than one

Just as there are different ways of thinking about division, there are different ways of thinking about fractions. For example, 12 cookies shared among 3 children is $\frac{12}{3} = 4$. This example is a rate, a partitive form of division: 12 for 3, or 4 for 1. The problem: 12 cookies, 3 to a bag, how many bags? can also be represented as $\frac{12}{3}$. But this example requires us to think about measurement. How many times does a group of 3 fit into 12? This is a quotative form of division. Fractions can be thought of similarly. Three submarine sandwiches shared among 4 people (partitive) is $\frac{3}{4}$, or $\frac{3}{4}$ for 1. In this case, $\frac{3}{4}$ can also be thought of as how many times a bar of 4 units fits into a bar of 3 units (quotative). Not once—only $\frac{3}{4}$ of the 4 fits.

When fractions are developed with fair-sharing division situations, it is easier for learners to construct the big idea that multiplication and division are related to fractions: 3 subs shared among 5 children results in each child getting $\frac{1}{5}$ of each sub. Because there are 3 subs, everyone gets $3 \times \frac{1}{5}$, or $\frac{3}{5}$. The idea of fractions as division is an important idea on the landscape. To deeply understand fractions, learners need to generalize the partitive and quotative relations: 1 candy bar shared among 8 children is equivalent to 1 out of 8 parts. Another way to think about this is to think of how 3 subs shared with 5 people (3 divided by 5) results in $\frac{3}{5}$ of one sub. Learners do not need to know the terms *partitive* and *quotative*, but they do need to know that 3 things shared among 5 people results in $\frac{3}{5}$. The slash symbol between the numerator and denominator is just a symbol to represent division.

❖ With unit fractions, the greater the denominator, the smaller the piece is

Students initially may think the reverse—that unit fractions with greater denominators represent greater amounts—because they attempt to generalize their knowledge of whole number to fractions. For example, they reason that since 8 is greater than 7, $\frac{1}{8}$ must be greater than $\frac{1}{7}$. When students are introduced to fractions in fair-sharing contexts, it is easy for them to understand that the greater the denominator, the smaller the piece. When eight people share a pizza, each piece is smaller than when seven people share it.

❖ Pieces don't have to be congruent to be equivalent

Fair-sharing contexts also provide learners with opportunities to explore how fractional parts can be equivalent without necessarily being congruent. They may look different but still be the same amount. For example, a square can be cut into two triangular halves (diagonally) or two rectangular halves (vertically). The pieces may look different, but the areas are equivalent.

❖ For equivalence, the ratio must be kept constant

Equivalence of fractions is often a difficult concept for students to understand. Traditionally, learners have been taught to make equivalent fractions by multiplying or dividing by one (in the form of $\frac{2}{2}$, $\frac{3}{3}$, etc.). Even when learners successfully use this strategy and can parrot back that they are multiplying by one, they may not be convinced that the fractions are really equivalent. Understanding that $\frac{6}{10}$ is not $\frac{3}{5}$ doubled requires that learners understand the implicit 2 for 1 ratio. Imagine a rectangle cut into tenths with six out of the ten shaded, as shown below. Establishing equivalence requires that every two become a new part (2 for 1). Then there are fifths (cut with the arrows) instead of tenths and only three shaded parts instead of six.

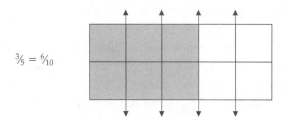

$$\frac{3}{5} = \frac{6}{10}$$

Fair sharing is a very helpful context for exploring equivalence because it is often easier for students to work with than the part-whole model. For example, it is much easier for learners to understand that 3 subs shared among 5 children is an equivalent situation to 6 subs shared among 10 children. If you double the number of people, you better double the number of subs! This is an example of keeping the ratio constant.

STRATEGIES

As you work with the activities in this unit, you will also notice that students will use many strategies to derive answers and to compare fractions. Here are some strategies to notice:

❖ **using landmark unit fractions or using common fractions**

❖ **using decimal and/or percentage equivalents**

❖ **using a ratio table as a tool to make equivalent fractions**

❖ **using multiplication and division to make equivalent fractions**

❖ **using a common whole to compare fractions**

❖ Using landmark unit fractions or using common fractions

When students are faced with fair-sharing situations, they will usually mathematize them in one of two ways. For example, when sharing subs they may use unit fractions (fractions with numerators of one) and cut one sub with landmark amounts first (such as $\frac{1}{2}$ or $\frac{1}{4}$) and continue with each sub and then try to add the amounts up (in the history of fractions this strategy is very similar to how early Egyptians thought about fractions). To represent sharing 3 subs among 5 people, students will usually do the following: Cut each sub in half. Everyone gets $\frac{1}{2}$. Cut the remaining $\frac{1}{2}$ up into fifths. This produces $\frac{1}{10}$ of a sub for each person. So everyone gets $\frac{1}{2} + \frac{1}{10}$.

The second strategy is different. It produces common fractions—in which the numerator is not one. Here each sub is cut into fifths at the start, since there are five people. Now everyone gets $3 \times \frac{1}{5}$, or $\frac{3}{5}$ of a sub.

Each of these strategies brings learners to different roadblocks. In both cases learners may struggle to determine what the total amount is. When using unit fractions, they must figure out how to add fractions with different denominators, and they must determine what to call $\frac{1}{5}$ of $\frac{1}{2}$. They are faced with the idea that the whole matters. They need to know what the whole is in order to name the part: is the fifth the whole, or is the sub the whole? is the sliver a fifth or a tenth? When using common fractions, students end up with $3 \times \frac{1}{5}$ and are faced with the relationship of division and multiplication: 3 subs divided by 5 people produces 1 divided by 5, times 3. They also encounter the relationship between partitive (fair sharing) and quotative (part-whole) representations of fractions and can be pushed to generalize about these relations.

❖ Using decimal and/or percentage equivalents

Some students may recognize the "3 subs for 5 people" situation as division and use the long division algorithm or grab a calculator. This move will result in a decimal quotient of 0.6. A few students may even turn this into a percentage equivalent and report that everyone gets 60 percent. In these cases, it is important to have them develop a justification for the equivalence using pictures of the sub. Can they show that 0.6, or 60 percent, is equivalent to 3/5? Justifying equivalence in a drawing (as on page 7) may become a roadblock. As you progress through this unit, look for opportunities for rich discussion around these strategies and big ideas and help students work through the roadblocks.

❖ Using a ratio table as a tool to make equivalent fractions

The fair-sharing situations in this unit help to generate use of the ratio table as a tool to make equivalent fractions. Students will notice patterns and develop strategies to make equivalent fractions. The first strategy you will most likely see is a doubling strategy. If you double the amount to be shared and you double the number of people, the result is the same. This strategy is very helpful in some cases, such as $\frac{3}{5} = \frac{6}{10} = \frac{?}{20}$, but it is not sufficient for all cases, for example when numbers are not as friendly. Students can also use the ratio table to keep rates equivalent by adding numerators and adding denominators. Three subs for 4 people and 6 subs for 8 people can be used to derive 9 subs for 12 people.

❖ Using multiplication and division to make equivalent fractions

Eventually students will construct the strategy of using multiplication and division to make equivalent fractions. For example, to find an equivalent for 3/5 with a denominator of 10, students must multiply the 3 by 2, since 10 divided by 5 equals 2, to produce 6; or students can divide the 10 by the 5 to produce 2 and then multiply the 3 by 2 to produce 6. Because fractions can be thought of as division and simplifying fractions is an important strategy for making equivalents, it is often a very efficient strategy to use even when dividing whole numbers. For example, 300 divided by 12 can be simplified to 100 divided by 4. The simplified version can be done mentally! This unit was carefully crafted and field-tested to ensure that simplifying is specifically addressed, both for fractions and for division with whole numbers. Not only will a discussion on this idea come up as students explore fair-sharing situations, but minilessons are also included to support the use of this strategy for whole-number division.

❖ Using a common whole to compare fractions

Comparing fractions creates another hurdle for students. How can they make a common whole to compare them? Initially, many numbers that are not common multiples may be tried as denominators. It is important to let students grapple with this problem. Eventually they will gravitate toward the realization that a common whole can be made by finding a common multiple. While a common multiple may be the result of their process, it is not important to name it as a common multiple at this time. By allowing their struggle and supporting their quest to find a common whole, you give students the opportunity to "own" the solution when they finally hit on the idea of common denominators.

MATHEMATICAL MODELING

Several mathematical models are developed in this unit, but only two are being introduced for the first time: the ratio table and the measurement model. With the ratio table model, students are supported to envision equivalent fair-sharing relationships. As the unit progresses, the ratio table model is used to support the development of various strategies for finding equivalent rates. Then the measurement model is introduced and equivalent fractions are explored with fraction bars and number lines.

Models go through three stages of development (Gravemeijer 1999; Fosnot and Dolk 2002):

❖ *model of the situation*

❖ *model of students' strategies*

❖ *model as a tool for thinking*

❖ Model of the situation

Initially models grow out of modeling the situation— in this unit, the ratio table emerges as a chart to ensure fair sharing during future field trips. The measurement model emerges as students design a 60k bike course.

❖ Model of students' strategies

Students benefit from seeing the teacher model their strategies. Once a model has been introduced as a model of the situation, you can use it to model students' strategies as they explain their thinking. If a student says, "I doubled the numerator and doubled the denominator," draw the following:

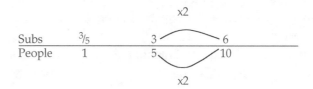

If a student says, "I added the 5 and 10 to make 15, so I added the 3 and 6 to make 9," draw the following:

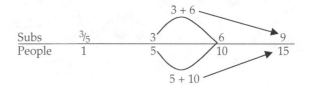

Representations like these give students a chance to discuss and envision each other's strategies.

❖ Model as a tool for thinking

Eventually learners become able to use the model as a tool to think with—they will be able to use it as a tool to prove and explore their ideas about proportional reasoning. Ratio tables can be presented as t-charts:

Number of Subs	Number of People
³⁄₅	1
3	5
6	10
9	15

Measurement models become number lines where fractions can be placed as numbers. In time, this model is very helpful for addition and subtraction of fractions. Although operations are not the focus of this unit, you may find some students beginning to explore that topic.

Many opportunities to discuss these landmarks will arise as you work through this unit. Look for moments of puzzlement. Don't hesitate to let students discuss their ideas and check and recheck their strategies. Celebrate their accomplishments—they are young mathematicians at work! A graphic of the full landscape of learning for fractions, decimals, and percents is provided on page 11. The purpose of the graphic is to allow you to see the longer journey of your students' mathematical development and to place your work with this unit within the scope of this long-term development. You may also find it helpful to use this graphic as a way to record the progress of individual students for yourself. Each landmark can be shaded in as you find evidence in a student's work and in what the student says—evidence that a landmark strategy, big idea, or way of modeling has been constructed. In a sense, you will be recording the individual pathways your students take as they develop as young mathematicians!

References and Resources

Dolk, Maarten and Catherine Twomey Fosnot. 2005. *Multiplication and Division Minilessons, Grades 3–5.* CD-ROM with accompanying facilitator's guide by Antonia Cameron, Carol Mosesson Teig, Sherrin B. Hersch, and Catherine Twomey Fosnot. Portsmouth, NH: Heinemann.

————. 2006a. *Fostering Children's Mathematical Development, Grades 5–8: The Landscape of Learning.* CD-ROM with accompanying facilitator's guide by Sherrin B. Hersch, Catherine Twomey Fosnot, and Antonia Cameron. Portsmouth, NH: Heinemann.

————. 2006b. *Sharing Submarine Sandwiches: A Context for Fractions, Grades 5–8.* CD-ROM with accompanying facilitator's guide by Sherrin B. Hersch, Catherine Twomey Fosnot, and Antonia Cameron. Portsmouth, NH: Heinemann.

Fosnot, Catherine Twomey and Maarten Dolk. 2002. *Young Mathematicians at Work: Constructing Fractions, Decimals, and Percents.* Portsmouth, NH: Heinemann.

Gravemeijer, Koeno P.E. 1999. How emergent models may foster the constitution of formal mathematics. *Mathematical Thinking and Learning, 1*(2), 155–77.

Hersh, Reuben. 1997. *What is Mathematics, Really?* London: Oxford University Press.

Streefland, Leen. 1991. *Fractions in Realistic Mathematics Education: A Paradigm of Developmental Research.* Dordrecht, Netherlands: Kluwer.

van Galen, Frans, Monica Wijers, Gail Burrill, and Mary S. Spence. 1997. *Mathematics in Context: Some of the Parts.* Orlando, FL: Holt, Rinehart, and Winston.

FRACTIONS, DECIMALS, and PERCENTS

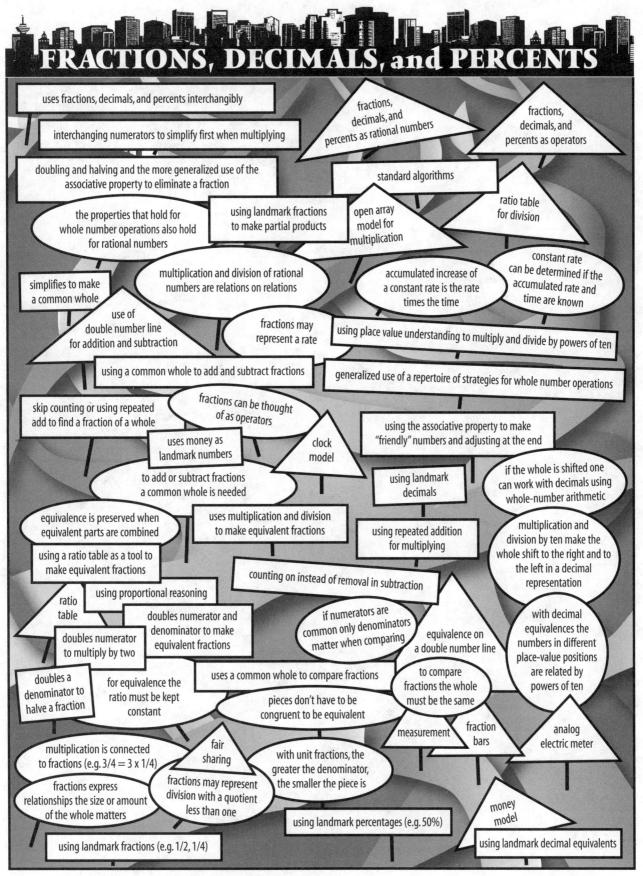

uses fractions, decimals, and percents interchangibly

interchanging numerators to simplify first when multiplying

doubling and halving and the more generalized use of the associative property to eliminate a fraction

fractions, decimals, and percents as rational numbers

fractions, decimals, and percents as operators

standard algorithms

ratio table for division

the properties that hold for whole number operations also hold for rational numbers

using landmark fractions to make partial products

open array model for multiplication

simplifies to make a common whole

multiplication and division of rational numbers are relations on relations

accumulated increase of a constant rate is the rate times the time

constant rate can be determined if the accumulated rate and time are known

use of double number line for addition and subtraction

fractions may represent a rate

using place value understanding to multiply and divide by powers of ten

using a common whole to add and subtract fractions

generalized use of a repertoire of strategies for whole number operations

skip counting or using repeated add to find a fraction of a whole

fractions can be thought of as operators

clock model

using the associative property to make "friendly" numbers and adjusting at the end

uses money as landmark numbers

using landmark decimals

if the whole is shifted one can work with decimals using whole-number arithmetic

to add or subtract fractions a common whole is needed

equivalence is preserved when equivalent parts are combined

uses multiplication and division to make equivalent fractions

using repeated addition for multiplying

multiplication and division by ten make the whole shift to the right and to the left in a decimal representation

using a ratio table as a tool to make equivalent fractions

counting on instead of removal in subtraction

ratio table

using proportional reasoning

doubles numerator and denominator to make equivalent fractions

if numerators are common only denominators matter when comparing

equivalence on a double number line

with decimal equivalences the numbers in different place-value positions are related by powers of ten

doubles numerator to multiply by two

doubles a denominator to halve a fraction

for equivalence the ratio must be kept constant

uses a common whole to compare fractions

to compare fractions the whole must be the same

pieces don't have to be congruent to be equivalent

measurement

fraction bars

analog electric meter

multiplication is connected to fractions (e.g. 3/4 = 3 x 1/4)

fair sharing

with unit fractions, the greater the denominator, the smaller the piece is

fractions express relationships the size or amount of the whole matters

fractions may represent division with a quotient less than one

money model

using landmark percentages (e.g. 50%)

using landmark decimal equivalents

using landmark fractions (e.g. 1/2, 1/4)

The landscape of learning: fractions, decimals, and percents on the horizon showing landmark strategies (rectangles), big ideas (ovals), and models (triangles).

DAY ONE
The Field Trip

Today, the context of fair-sharing submarine sandwiches is introduced to support the development of several big ideas related to fractions. Students explore four situations: 3 subs shared by 4 people, 4 subs shared by 5 people, 7 subs shared by 8 people, and 3 subs shared by 5 people. Students work with partners to determine how much of a sub each person in each of these groups receives. They then make posters of some of the ideas they want to share in a math congress, to be held on Day Two.

Day One Outline

Developing the Context

☀ Tell the story about the distribution of submarine sandwiches on a field trip.

☀ Ask students to work in pairs to determine if the distribution was fair and to figure out what portion of a sandwich each person received.

Supporting the Investigation

☀ Note students' strategies as they investigate how much of a sub each person received.

☀ Ensure that they indicate where the subs should be cut.

☀ Support students as they move on to figure out which group received the most to eat.

Preparing for the Math Congress

☀ Have students make posters of the ideas and strategies they want to present during the math congress on Day Two.

☀ Review students' posters to determine who you will have share during the congress and what strategies you will highlight.

Materials Needed

Field trip posters [If you do not have the full-color posters (available from Heinemann), you can use the smaller black-and-white versions in Appendix A.]

Large chart paper— a few sheets per pair of students

Connecting cubes—one bin per pair of students

Calculators, as needed

Markers

Developing the Context

☀ Tell the story about the distribution of submarine sandwiches on a field trip.

☀ Ask students to work in pairs to determine if the distribution was fair and to figure out what portion of a sandwich each person received.

Display the four field trip posters (or Appendix A) as you tell the following story:

A fifth-grade class traveled on a field trip in four separate cars. The school provided a lunch of submarine sandwiches for each group. When they stopped for lunch, the subs were cut and shared as follows:

- *The first group had 4 people and shared 3 subs equally.*

- *The second group had 5 people and shared 4 subs equally.*

- *The third group had 8 people and shared 7 subs equally.*

- *The last group had 5 people and shared 3 subs equally.*

When they returned from the field trip, the children began to argue that the distribution of sandwiches had not been fair, that some children got more to eat than the others. Were they right? Or did everyone get the same amount?

Facilitate a preliminary discussion in the meeting area before the students set off to work. Allow students to share their initial thoughts and then ask them to work in pairs to investigate these questions:

1. Was the distribution fair—did each person in each group get the same amount?

2. How much of a sub did each person get, assuming the pieces were cut equally?

Behind the Numbers

The numbers in this story have been chosen purposefully. Many students initially think that 3 subs for 4 people, 4 subs for 5 people, and 7 subs for 8 people are equivalent situations since there is always 1 sub fewer than the number of people. They will usually also argue that 3 subs for 4 people is not equivalent to 3 subs for 5 people, because more people are sharing when there are 5 and thus the pieces are smaller. When students go off to investigate, they will be surprised to discover that the first three situations are not equivalent. But they are correct about the fourth situation, and this beginning notion of fractions as division will be deepened as you proceed through the unit. Given these specific numbers in the context, students' conceptions at the start regarding proportional reasoning are illuminated. Don't try to dissuade them of their convictions at this point. Just facilitate a discussion and then let them work in pairs to figure out how much each person in each group received. Use the discussion as a motivator for inquiry and let them be surprised at the results.

Supporting the Investigation

☀ Note students' strategies as they investigate how much of a sub each person received.

☀ Ensure that they indicate where the subs should be cut.

☀ Support students as they move on to figure out which group received the most to eat.

Assign math partners and give each pair of students some large chart paper. Have calculators and bins of connecting cubes available so that students may use them if they wish. Confer with students as needed to support and challenge.

Conferring with Students at Work

Gabrielle: Three subs for 5 people. I think we should cut each sub in half first.

Michael: OK. *(Makes a line through each of three subs at the halfway point, producing six halves.)* But there are only 5 people. What do we do with this last half?

Gabrielle: Let's cut that up into 5 pieces. There. So everyone in this car got ½ + ⅕. Now let's do 3 subs for 4.

Caroline (the teacher)**:** *(pointing to the small sliver)* Tell me about this piece.

Gabrielle: We cut it into 5 pieces so everyone could have a piece of what was left.

Caroline: I see that you wrote ⅕ on your paper. Is this ⅕ of a sub?

Gabrielle: Oh… No. It is ⅕ of the half.

Caroline: Hmmm…⅕ of ½? I wonder how much of the whole sub that is?

Author's Notes

Move around the room, noting the strategies being used. Confer with a few groups as they work.

Many students will start by cutting the sandwiches into large landmark pieces such as halves or thirds. When faced with the leftover pieces, they will then cut slivers and struggle with what to name those pieces.

By staying grounded in the context of the sandwich, Caroline encourages the students to realize that the size of the whole matters: ⅕ of a half is not the same as ⅕ of a sandwich.

By asking the students to reflect on how many slivers (⅕ of ½) will fit in the whole sandwich, Caroline supports them to realize that if the other half were cut similarly there would be ten slivers. She helps them to realize that ⅕ of ½ is ¹⁄₁₀.

Take note of the various struggles and strategies you see as students investigate how much of a sub each person got. Encourage struggles to become beautiful inquiries! As students cut up the subs, you might see them

✦ cut each sub into landmark fractions first, such as halves or thirds, and then cut the remainder into slivers. This strategy may cause them to struggle with what to name each piece: What do you call ⅕ of a half? *[See Figure 1, page 16]*

✦ cut each sub into a number of pieces that is the same as the number of people. For example, when sharing 3 subs among 5 people, each of the 3 subs is cut into 5 pieces, resulting in ⅕ of each sub per student, or 3 × ⅕. This strategy may cause students to struggle with the notion that fractions are relations and that the size or amount of the whole matters. Everyone gets ³⁄₁₅ of the pieces, but this

Behind the Numbers

When they begin to compare and/or add pieces together, some students may attempt to represent subs with the connecting cubes, but may not make equal size subs. If you see students using various sizes, be sure to point this out by asking if one group received bigger subs. Stay grounded in the context to help students realize the meaning of what they are doing. As students struggle to ensure that the subs are all the same size, they will need to grapple with what numbers would be easy to use for the size of a common-length sub in order to compare and/or add the fractional amounts. Ten cubes may work nicely for fifths, but not so nicely for fourths or eighths! This inquiry will push students toward constructing the idea that a common multiple would be helpful. This idea is important for the construction of common denominators.

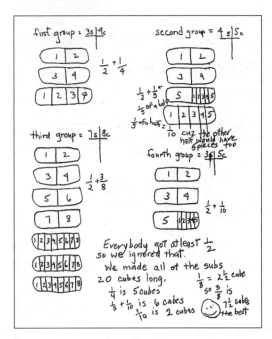

Figure 1

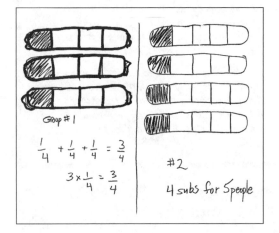

Figure 2

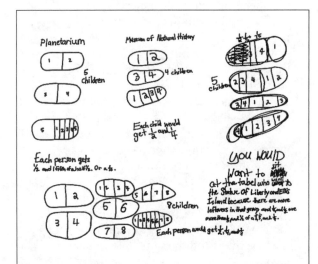

Figure 3

amount is also ⅗ of one sub. Students may also notice that fractions can be thought of as division: 3 subs shared by 5 people results in ⅗, or 3 × ⅕. *[See Figure 2]*

✦ use the long division algorithm or a calculator to derive a decimal quotient: 3 divided by 5 equals 0.6. This strategy often prompts students to inquire about equivalence, "How is it that some students got ⅗ and I got 0.6?" Encourage students to consider whether one answer is wrong or whether they are equivalent.

Ensure that all students indicate where the cuts would be made. If some students use a calculator to derive, for example, a quotient of 0.6 for 3 divided by 5, ask them to determine where the decimal equivalent would be on their drawing of the submarine sandwich. If they have not worked with decimals prior to this unit and they ask you what the decimal point means, you can tell them that 0.6 means six-tenths and then encourage them to think of the sandwiches in tenths.

Once students have cut up or shared the subs, they have to compare the results to determine which group got the most. Here you might see students

✦ work with unit fractions and ignore equivalent amounts:
  1. three subs for 4 people is ½ + ¼
  2. four subs for 5 people is ½ + ⅕ + ⅒
  3. seven subs for 8 people is ½ + ¼ + ⅛
  4. three subs for 5 people is ½ + ⅒

In each case everyone got at least ½, so those halves can be ignored when comparing the situations. Group #3 received ⅛ more per person than group #1, and group #2 received ⅕ more per person than group #4. Hence, groups #1 and #4 can be ruled out and only groups #2 and #3 need to be compared to determine which of the four groups got the most. This strategy brings students nicely to examining denominators as divisors. One sub shared by 4 people results in larger pieces than 1 sub shared by 5 people! Similarly, ⅛ is a larger piece than ⅒. When comparing unit fractions, the greater the denominator, the smaller the piece is. *[See Figure 3]*

✦ compare common fractions or decimal equivalents by finding a common whole.

If students have divided each sub by the number of people in the group, they have obtained $\frac{3}{4}$, $\frac{4}{5}$, $\frac{7}{8}$, and $\frac{3}{5}$ (or decimal equivalents) and now they have to compare those fractions. This strategy usually produces an inquiry about what size to make the subs so that they can be compared. At first, students may simply use trial and error, but eventually they will recognize that it is easier to use a common multiple of the number of people (a common denominator). *[See Figure 4]*

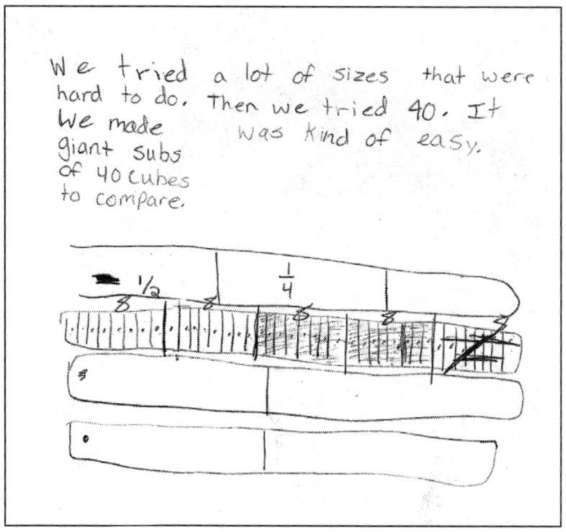
We tried a lot of sizes that were hard to do. Then we tried 40. It was kind of easy.
We made giant subs of 40 cubes to compare.
1/2
1/4

Figure 4

Preparing for the Math Congress

After a sufficient amount of time has been devoted to the investigation, ask students to make posters in preparation for the math congress to be held on Day Two. Explain that the posters need to be clear for others to understand. They should not be just students' draft notes copied over. They should be concise and clear presentations of the important ideas and strategies students want to present.

Mathematicians write up their mathematics for math journals. In these articles, they do not merely reiterate everything they did. Instead, they craft a proof or argument for other mathematicians. Doing this not only generates further reflection, it focuses the author on developing a convincing and elegant argument—an important part of mathematics. Of course, elementary students are not expected to write formal proofs, but by focusing on the justification and logic of their arguments you are helping them develop the ability to write up their ideas for presentation in a mathematical community. For example, if students have constructed the idea that fractions are division, that 3 subs for 5 children is $\frac{3}{5}$ of a sub for each child, push them to generalize the idea and suggest that they focus their poster on proving this generalization.

- Have students make posters of the ideas and strategies they want to present during the math congress on Day Two.
- Review students' posters to determine who you will have share during the congress and what strategies you will highlight.

Tips for Structuring the Math Congress

Plan on structuring a congress to discuss some of the big ideas related to fractions. Examine the posters as you plan for the congress and think about how you want the conversation to flow. By noting students' struggles and strategies, you can make a decision regarding which students you will ask to share and the strategies you will highlight. You will want to be sure to discuss the idea that fractions can be thought of as division: 3 subs shared by 5 people results in $\frac{3}{5}$ of a sub per person.

Usually, some student work will also illustrate a unit fraction strategy. Highlighting such a strategy will generate discussion of big ideas such as the following:

- the size or amount of the whole matters
- with unit fractions, the greater the denominator, the smaller the piece is
- when naming the piece, the whole matters (what to call $\frac{1}{5}$ of $\frac{1}{2}$, etc.)

Reflections on the Day

Several big ideas about fractions were explored today as students investigated the fair-sharing situation. Some groups grappled with how to compare the amounts and developed a beginning understanding of common denominators. Others grappled with equivalence, for example, what to call $\frac{1}{5}$ of $\frac{1}{2}$. Some realized that with unit fractions, the greater the denominator, the smaller the piece is. Still others, using a division strategy, determined that 3 subs shared by 5 people results in $\frac{3}{5}$ of one sub per person and they worked to generalize this idea.

DAY TWO
The Field Trip

The math workshop begins today with a display of the posters from Day One and a "gallery walk" during which students are encouraged to review all the posters and note their comments and questions. Discussion in the subsequent math congress focuses on several big ideas related to fractions.

Day Two Outline

Preparing for the Math Congress (continued from Day One)

☀ Conduct a gallery walk for students to review and post comments on each other's posters.

Facilitating the Math Congress

☀ Focus the congress on big ideas such as fractions as division, equivalence, and/or what to name a piece.

Materials Needed

Students' posters from Day One

Before class, display all the posters around the meeting area.

Sticky notes—one pad per student

Large chart pad and easel (or chalkboard or whiteboard)

Markers

Preparing for the Math Congress (continued from Day One)

☀ Conduct a gallery walk for students to review and post comments on each other's posters.

Explain to students that before you start the math congress, you are going to have a gallery walk to look at the posters from Day One. Pass out small pads of sticky notes and suggest that students use them to record comments or questions. These notes can be placed directly on the posters. Give students about fifteen minutes to read and comment on the mathematics on the posters. Then, give everyone a few minutes to read the sticky notes on their own posters before you start the math congress.

Facilitating the Math Congress

☀ Focus the congress on big ideas such as fractions as division, equivalence, and/or what to name a piece.

Convene the students in a meeting area to discuss a few of the ideas on the posters. Rather than having students just share the strategies they used, look for some big ideas to focus conversation on, such as fractions as division, equivalence, or what to name a piece.

Inside One Classroom

A Portion of the Math Congress

Caroline (the teacher): Let's start with you, Jennifer and John. You are pretty excited about something you noticed, right? Let's discuss it.

Jennifer: The answers were in the problem! We noticed that 3 subs for 4 people equaled ¾, and it kept going like that! Three for 5 was ⅗.

Gabrielle: I noticed that on your poster when I walked around, but I don't get it. Why did that happen? Michael and I got different answers.

John: It's kind of like an array. Three subs for 4 people. If you cut each sub up into fourths, everybody gets ¼ of each sub. But there are 3 subs. So it is $3 \times \frac{1}{4}$.

Caroline: How many people can put in their own words what John and Jennifer are talking about? What do they mean, "like an array?" Josh?

Josh: Wow. I get it. That is so cool. The fourths are in a column.

Gabrielle: Does that happen every time?

Author's Notes

Caroline starts by asking the students to come up and share the generalization they have been working to prove. This move implicitly suggests that part of doing mathematics is communicating and justifying thinking to a community of other mathematicians.

Discussion is welcomed.

Asking for clarification and paraphrasing ensures that students understand each other's ideas and can discuss them.

continued on next page

continued from previous page

Jennifer: Yes. See. Here's 7 for 8. Cut it into the number of people, 8. Everybody gets $\frac{1}{8}$. But there are 7 subs, so $7 \times \frac{1}{8}$. That's $\frac{7}{8}$.

Students, not the teacher, defend their thinking.

Caroline: Will this always happen? Can we generalize? If we have a certain number of things and we share them among a certain number of groups, will the answer always be the number of things over the number of groups?

Caroline pushes the community to generalize—to explain why.

Yolanda: It is like that! It is just like division! Twelve cookies shared by 3 kids is $\frac{12}{3}$. The bar just means divide. Three subs shared by 5 people is just 3 divided by 5, and that is what the bar means!

Caroline: Gabrielle, what do you think? Do you agree?

Caroline returns to Gabrielle to see if she has been convinced. Knowledge holds up in this community if and only if the entire community accepts it.

Gabrielle: Yes. They convinced me. But why don't our answers match? What's wrong with what Michael and I did? I'm sure our way works, too, but our answers are different.

Caroline: Tell us about your strategy.

Caroline encourages a look at other strategies and shifts the conversation to equivalence. By exploring a strategy in which landmark unit fractions have been used and asking students to compare it to a common fraction use (such as John's and Jennifer's strategy), Caroline makes equivalence the new focus of discussion.

Gabrielle: *(Tapes the poster to the chalkboard.)* We cut each sandwich into halves, passed those out, and then cut the rest up into smaller pieces.

Caroline: Why don't you walk us through how you did 7 subs for 8 people.

Gabrielle: We cut 4 subs into halves and everybody got $\frac{1}{2}$. The next 2 subs we cut into fourths. And then the last sub we cut into eighths. So everyone in that car got $\frac{1}{2} + \frac{1}{4} + \frac{1}{8}$.

Caroline: How many people can put in their own words what Michael and Gabrielle did? Turn to the person next to you and discuss Michael and Gabrielle's strategy. *(Allows a few minutes for pair talk.)* So are they both right? Why don't the answers match?

Pair talk is used to engage all the students in considering equivalence.

Gabrielle: I think we are both right. Because $\frac{1}{2}$ is equal to $\frac{4}{8}$ *(Draws lines through the half as she talks.)* And $\frac{1}{4}$ is equal to $\frac{2}{8}$. So $\frac{1}{8}$ more is $\frac{7}{8}$!

Caroline: *(Writing the equation as she talks.)* So $\frac{1}{2} + \frac{1}{4} + \frac{1}{8} = \frac{4}{8} + \frac{2}{8} + \frac{1}{8}$. They both equal $\frac{7}{8}$. You convinced me, Gabrielle! How about the rest of you? *(Several nods of agreement.)* Turning all the pieces into eighths was a great idea, wasn't it? For homework tonight, I would like you to make up a scenario like this, where a certain number of things is going to be shared among a number of people. You can pick the numbers. Solve it two ways, like John and Jennifer did and like Gabrielle and Michael did, and then show how the answers are equivalent.

The students must justify their arguments and convince the community.

Homework is structured to provide more reflection on the issues that have been discussed. Alternative strategies are accepted and valued.

■ Assessment Tips

It would be nice to place the posters in students' portfolios; however, they are probably too large. If so, you can take a photograph of each poster and staple it to a blank page for your anecdotal notes. Make notes about the strategies and big ideas described in the introduction to this unit (pages 6–9). Do you have evidence that any of these ideas and strategies have been constructed?

Reflections on the Day

Today students discussed fractions as division. They realized that 3 subs for 5 people can be mathematized as 3 divided by 5, which results in $\frac{3}{5}$ of 1 sub per person, or $3 \times \frac{1}{5}$. They also discussed various ways to compare the amounts to determine which amount was the greatest, and they considered strategies for determining equivalent fractions.

DAY THREE
Redistributing

Today's math workshop begins with a warm-up minilesson on multiplication, using a string of related problems designed to encourage the use of partial products and to revisit the idea of fractions as division. Students then begin an investigation involving redistributing: they examine if the distribution would have been more equitable if groups #1 and #3 had combined and shared their subs, and if groups #2 and #4 did the same. Students are asked to determine how much each person would have received in this new scenario.

Note: It is not necessary to use the word *redistributing* with your students. You might prefer to use terms like *sharing differently*.

Day Three Outline

Minilesson: A Multiplication String

☀ Work on a string of related problems designed to encourage the use of partial products.

☀ Record students' strategies on an open array.

Developing the Context

☀ Display the field trip posters again and ask students if it would have been fairer if groups #1 and #3 had combined and shared, and groups #2 and #4 had combined and shared.

Supporting the Investigation

☀ Note students' strategies as they investigate the combined-group sharing.

Preparing for the Math Congress

☀ Have students make posters of the important ideas they developed as they investigated the combined-group sharing.

Materials Needed

Field trip posters (or Appendix A)

Connecting cubes—one bin per pair of students

Calculators, as needed

Large chart paper—a few sheets per pair of students

Large chart pad and easel

Markers

Minilesson: A Multiplication String (10–15 minutes)

☀ Work on a string of related problems designed to encourage the use of partial products.

☀ Record students' strategies on an open array.

This mental math minilesson uses a string of related problems designed to encourage students to examine partial products and to compose and decompose with them. Do one problem at a time and record students' strategies on an open array (see Inside One Classroom below). Invite students to discuss the connection with their work on Day Two.

String of related problems:

$$10 \times 127$$
$$127 \times 2$$
$$127 \times 12$$
$$44 \times 10$$
$$44 \times 9$$
$$3 \times \tfrac{1}{5}$$
$$7 \times \tfrac{1}{8}$$
$$3 \times \tfrac{1}{4}$$
$$4 \times \tfrac{1}{5}$$

Behind the Numbers

The first two problems in the string will probably be easy for your students. The third problem is more difficult, but the products of the first two can be used to derive the third. The fifth can be done by using the fourth and removing a group of 44. It is assumed that students will be quite comfortable at this point with using distributivity. The first five problems encourage students to think about this idea and connect it to the fraction work they did on Days One and Two. Three subs shared by 5 children was $3 \times \tfrac{1}{5}$, or $\tfrac{1}{5} + \tfrac{1}{5} + \tfrac{1}{5}$.

A Portion of the Minilesson

Inside One Classroom

Caroline (the teacher): Here's our first warm-up problem: 10×127. Thumbs-up when you have an answer. Michael?

Michael: 1270. I just know. I used the pattern of multiplying by ten.

Caroline: *(Draws the following representation of Michael's strategy.)*

	127
10	1270

Does everyone agree with Michael? *(No disagreement is apparent.)* 127 tens? OK. Let's go to the next one: 127×2. Emmy?

Author's Notes

Caroline begins with two problems that are quite easy for the students. She uses them only to get up the partial products that may be used for the third problem.

The arrays are drawn to provide an image of the strategy for discussion. The students are not expected to draw the arrays, but over time the model will become a tool to think with.

continued on next page

continued from previous page

Emmy: It's 254. I doubled the 100 and then doubled the 27.

Caroline: How many people did it like Emmy? *(Several hands go up.)*
  What other ways are there? Sean?

Sean: I thought of it as 125 twice, like a dollar and a quarter.
  So 250, plus 4.

Caroline: What do you think? Does Sean's way work?
  I'll make the array.

	125	2
2	250	4

Suzanne: Yes. He just broke up the pieces differently than Emmy.

Caroline: OK. Let's try this one: 12×127. You can keep track on
  paper if you need to. Remember, mental math doesn't have to be in
  your head, just with your head!

Kathie: I just put the last two problems together.

Caroline: Nice. I'll make a picture of what you said.

	127
10	1270
2	254

Caroline uses the open array to represent Kathie's use of the partial products.

Caroline: Here's our next one: 10×44. And since I know you all
  know this one, I'll just make a picture. See if you can use the picture
  to do 9×44.

	44
10	440

The array model provides a focus of discussion. Deciding what to remove is difficult and here the students are encouraged to reflect with pair talk.

Amanda: I think you take a group of ten away.

Caroline: *(Draws a picture.)* What do you all think? Is Amanda right, a
  group of ten? Turn to the person next to you and talk about this.

	44	-1
10	440 – 10	

Discussing each other's strategies fosters a sense of risk-taking and community.

Sean: No, I think it has to be a group of 44 that gets removed. The line
  needs to go across the bottom. We need 9 rows of 44, not 10 rows
  of 43.

continued on next page

continued from previous page

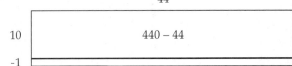

Caroline: Everyone agrees with Sean? *(Heads nod.)* OK. I'm wondering about what we did yesterday and what that would look like on the array. How about $3 \times \frac{1}{5}$?

Michael: I know the answer is $\frac{3}{5}$. But what would it look like on the array?

Caroline: Like this.

Having brought up distributivity, Caroline now moves to fractions. By using the same numbers as the day before, she supports students to consider how $3 \times \frac{1}{5}$ might be represented in an array with partial products.

Several students: Oh, I get it. It is $\frac{1}{5} + \frac{1}{5} + \frac{1}{5}$. $\frac{3}{5}$. Just like the subs.

Developing the Context

☀ Display the field trip posters again and ask students if it would have been fairer if groups #1 and #3 had combined and shared, and groups #2 and #4 had combined and shared.

After the minilesson, display the four field trip posters again (or Appendix A) and remind students of their answers from the investigation on Day Two:

1. Three subs for 4 people is $\frac{1}{2} + \frac{1}{4}$, or $\frac{3}{4}$, so 4 people each got $\frac{3}{4}$ of a sub

2. Four subs for 5 people is $\frac{1}{2} + \frac{1}{5} + \frac{1}{10}$, or $\frac{4}{5}$, so 5 people each got $\frac{4}{5}$ of a sub

3. Seven subs for 8 people is $\frac{1}{2} + \frac{1}{4} + \frac{1}{8}$, or $\frac{7}{8}$, so 8 people each got $\frac{7}{8}$ of a sub

4. Three subs for 5 people is $\frac{1}{2} + \frac{1}{10}$, or $\frac{3}{5}$, so 5 people each got $\frac{3}{5}$ of a sub

Ask students to investigate if it would it have been fairer if groups #1 and #3 had combined and shared, and groups #2 and #4 had combined and shared. Place the related posters next to each other as you frame the question.

Behind the Numbers

Because there are not equal numbers of children in each group, this investigation cannot be solved by simply averaging the fractions—the fractions cannot just be added up and divided by two because there are two groups. This is a weighted average situation—the subs need to be redistributed to the number of children, not the number of groups. Solving the problem in this way results in 10 subs shared by 12 children (groups #1 and #3) and 7 subs shared by 10 children (groups #2 and #4).

Supporting the Investigation

Assign math partners and give each pair of students some large chart paper. Have calculators and bins of connecting cubes available so that students may use them if they wish. Confer with students as needed to support and challenge.

☀ Note students' strategies as they investigate the combined-group sharing.

Inside One Classroom

Conferring with Students at Work

Author's Notes

Sophie: Three subs for 4 people and 7 for 8. That's ¾ and ⅞. I don't know how to add these. How do you add fractions?

Samantha: No, we don't add the fractions. We have to add the subs and share them. And we have to add the people, too.

Sophie: Ok. So that's 10 subs for 12 people?

Samantha: Yep. I'll draw the subs. *(Draws 10 subs and cuts 6 of them in half.)*

Move around the room and note the strategies being used. Confer with a few groups as they work.

Caroline (the teacher)**:** And why wouldn't that be adding the fractions?

Samantha: Because, if you added ¾ and ⅞ you would get a lot more. You would get more than a whole sub I think. And there's not enough for that.

Some students may first think they have to add the fractions. By pushing students to realize that more than a whole sub would be the result, Caroline helps them realize that they are not adding, but redistributing.

Caroline: Sophie, do you agree?

Sophie: Yes. She's right. It would be more than a whole sub. ⅞ is almost a whole sub. And ¾ is a half and a quarter.

Caroline: How many eighths are there in a ¼?

Sophie: Two, I think. Yes. Because …⅛ is half of a ¼?

Caroline: Hmmm….so if we did add these, we would have $\frac{7}{8} + \frac{1}{8} + \frac{1}{2} + \frac{1}{8}$.

Caroline supports them to move to a landmark whole.

Sophie: Yep, way too much. We're not adding. We're sharing. So I think it has to be in between ¾ and ⅞. Seven subs for 8 people was the most before. Now they have to give a little of theirs to the other group

By staying grounded in the context of the sandwich Caroline encourages the students to realize the meaning of what they are doing.

Take note of the various struggles and strategies you see as students work to figure out how much of a sub each person receives when the groups are combined. Encourage struggles to become fun challenges! As students cut up the subs, you might notice them:

+ cutting halves and using unit landmark fractions.

Figure 5

For groups #2 and #4—7 subs for 10 people—students might cut 5 subs into halves and then cut the remaining 2 subs into fifths, resulting in $\frac{1}{2} + \frac{1}{5}$ per person. Recall that when there were four groups, the people in group #2 each received $\frac{1}{2} + \frac{1}{5} + \frac{1}{10}$, and the people in group #4 each received $\frac{1}{2} + \frac{1}{10}$. The extra $\frac{1}{5}$ that each person in group #2 had then is now redistributed, some of it going to the members of group #4.

For groups #1 and #3—10 subs for 12 people—students might cut 6 subs into halves and then cut the remaining 4 subs into thirds, resulting in $\frac{1}{2} + \frac{1}{3}$. This strategy allows them to revisit the idea that when the numerators are the same, one only has to look at the denominators to compare the fractions. One sub for 5 people ($\frac{1}{5}$) is not as good a situation as 1 sub for 3 people ($\frac{1}{3}$), hence $\frac{1}{5} < \frac{1}{3}$. On the other hand, when compared to Day One, this situation is fairer. Each person in group #1 previously received $\frac{1}{2} + \frac{1}{4}$ and each person in group #3 previously received $\frac{1}{2} + \frac{1}{4} + \frac{1}{8}$. The extra $\frac{1}{8}$ per person has now been redistributed and the fourths have become thirds. *[See Figure 5]*

+ reflecting on the discussion of division from Day Two (cutting each sub into the same number of pieces as people) and realizing they now have

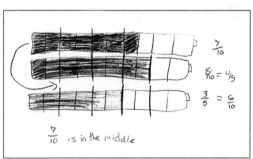

Figure 6

$\frac{7}{10}$ and $\frac{10}{12}$. This strategy requires students to consider how to compare these new amounts with the amounts from Day One: $\frac{3}{4}$ (group #1), $\frac{4}{5}$ (group #2), $\frac{7}{8}$ (group #3), and $\frac{3}{5}$ (group #4). Students will probably not be able to consider common denominators for all of these simultaneously, but they will have some informal ways to begin the comparison. For example, $\frac{4}{5}$ and $\frac{3}{5}$ might be compared to $\frac{7}{10}$ by drawing a picture or making a sub with ten connecting cubes and thinking of $\frac{7}{10}$ as $3\frac{1}{2}/5$, or $\frac{8}{10}$ as $\frac{4}{5}$ and $\frac{6}{10}$ as $\frac{3}{5}$. Now the $\frac{7}{10}$ can be seen as an amount right in between. *[See Figure 6]*

+ using the long division algorithm or a calculator to derive decimal quotients and then comparing them. This strategy produces nice equivalents for comparison. For example, $\frac{4}{5}$ and $\frac{3}{5}$ can be compared as 0.8 and 0.6, and 0.7 can then be explored as being in between. You may need to remind students that these decimal numbers represent tenths.

Don't discourage students from thinking of ratios such as $3\frac{1}{2}/5$. Some teachers think they should allow students to write fractions only in common forms, such as $\frac{7}{10}$. On the contrary, making equivalent relations is critical to developing numeracy and this ability to think flexibly is an important quality you want to support. Students who can think about the equivalence of these relations are learning to think like mathematicians!

Preparing for the Math Congress

After a sufficient amount of time has been devoted to the investigation, ask students to make posters in preparation for the math congress to be held on Day Four. Explain that the posters need to be clear for others to understand. They should not just be students' draft notes copied over. They should be concise and clear presentations of the important points students want to present: the method they used to compare the situations and a justification for why they think the combined-group sharing is fairer (or not).

☀ Have students make posters of the important ideas they developed as they investigated the combined-group sharing.

Reflections on the Day

The minilesson today encouraged students to use partial products when multiplying and to continue to think about fractions as division and the connection of this operation to multiplication: $\frac{3}{5} = 3 \times \frac{1}{5} = \frac{1}{5} + \frac{1}{5} + \frac{1}{5}$. The investigation also encouraged redistributing. Many students develop misconceptions about adding fractions, thinking that numerators can be added and denominators can be added. For example, they might think that $\frac{1}{3} + \frac{1}{2}$ is equivalent to $\frac{2}{5}$. Today you hit this misconception head-on to stop it from developing. Students investigated redistributing and discovered that it produces a fraction in between the two numbers; it does not produce a sum of the two numbers. By exploring this procedure in context and examining the results, students are supported to develop deep understandings about fractions, thereby avoiding common misconceptions.

Redistributing

Materials Needed

Calculator

Students' posters from Day Three

Large chart pad and easel

Markers

In today's minilesson, students investigate the fair sharing of money and explore how adding a dollar (in the numerator) and adding a person (in the denominator) do not establish an equivalent relation but in fact produce an increasingly greater result for each. Then students meet in small groups to discuss the strategies used during the investigation on Day Three. A math congress follows to continue discussion of redistributing.

Day Four Outline

Minilesson: Pass the Calculator

☀ Have students use a calculator to solve a string of related problems designed to highlight a common misconception regarding proportional reasoning

Preparing for the Math Congress (continued from Day Three)

☀ Have students meet in small groups to share their posters.

☀ Listen to some of their conversations for ideas and strategies that should be discussed in the math congress.

Facilitating the Math Congress

☀ Have students discuss their strategies for the combined-group sharing investigations.

☀ Ensure that students understand that they have been redistributing and sharing, not adding fractions.

Minilesson: Pass the Calculator (10–15 minutes)

This minilesson uses a calculator. Have the students sit in a circle and pass the calculator around. Start by having the first student divide $1 by 2 people and tell how much each person gets. The next student divides $2 by 3 people; the next $3 by 4 people; the next $4 by 5 people, continuing on around the circle. Record the results on a chart.

☀ Have students use a calculator to solve a string of related problems designed to highlight a common misconception regarding proportional reasoning.

String of related problems:

$$\tfrac{1}{2} = 0.50$$
$$\tfrac{2}{3} = 0.\overline{66}$$
$$\tfrac{3}{4} = 0.75$$
$$\tfrac{4}{5} = 0.80$$
$$\tfrac{5}{6} =$$
$$\tfrac{6}{7} =$$

etc.

Behind the Numbers

Have students discuss and generalize about what is happening and why. The results are becoming larger. Discuss how this might be connected to the field trip investigation. Remind them that the scenario of 7 subs for 8 people was more than 4 subs for 5 people or 3 subs for 4 people. Discuss what they think would have happened if there were 8 subs for 9 people, etc.

Preparing for the Math Congress
(continued from Day Three)

Have the students take out their posters from Day Three and then convene three or four small groups. Appoint one student in each group to facilitate and have the students discuss their strategies. As they share, listen in for important ideas that might be worth discussing further in the math congress, such as the following:

☀ Have students meet in small groups to share their posters.

☀ Listen to some of their conversations for ideas and strategies that should be discussed in the math congress.

+ how to compare fractions

+ interesting ways to redistribute

+ how they know that given two fractions, combining the groups represented by the numerators and combining the groups represented by the denominators produces a fraction in between

▪ Tips for Structuring the Math Congress

Look for evidence of two or three different approaches, such as the following:

+ cutting halves and using unit landmark fractions, redistributing the pieces, and realizing that the redistributing produced an amount in between

+ comparing common fractions and realizing that the redistributing produced a fraction in between the two original fractions

+ using the calculator or doing long division to produce decimal quotients, ordering the decimals, and realizing that the new amounts are numbers in between the original values

Plan to have two or three pairs of students whose work epitomizes these strategies share their solutions. Be prepared to discuss how the strategies are related and to examine the results and the arguments for determining if the combined-group situation is fairer.

Facilitating the Math Congress

☀ Have students discuss their strategies for the combined-group sharing investigations.

☀ Ensure that students understand that they have been redistributing and sharing, not adding fractions.

After sufficient small-group discussion, convene students in the meeting area to discuss a few of the strategies they used or important insights or ideas they had. The main objective of the congress is to establish that the redistributing did produce a situation that was somewhat fairer. Groups that initially had the most now have a bit less and groups that had the least now have a bit more. This conclusion, however, is not as important as the arguments students have for why this is so, the strategies they have used to determine the shares, and the approaches they have used to compare. It is also important to ensure that students understand that they have been redistributing and sharing, not adding fractions.

Reflections on the Day

As the investigation of the redistributing of the subs progressed, students examined ways to share the subs more fairly and they worked with landmark fractions to develop a sense of the relative magnitude of messier fractions. When adding fractions, students often add the numerators and denominators. Today students realized that doing this does not produce the addition of the fractional pieces, but instead produces a fraction in between.

Working with Landmarks

The focus today is on estimating or approximating landmark fractions to develop a sense of reasonableness, specifically when exploring the magnitude of the messy fraction $\frac{17}{22}$. Students are asked to determine how much everyone would have received if all the subs had been shared fairly among all the children: 17 subs for 22 children. Students work in pairs estimating this amount in relation to landmarks such as $\frac{1}{2}$ or $\frac{1}{4}$ and then make posters for a congress to be held on Day Six.

Day Five Outline

Developing the Context

☀ Display the field trip posters and summarize what students have discovered thus far.

☀ Ask students to investigate how much of a sub each person would have received if the 17 subs had been shared equally among all 22 people.

Supporting the Investigation

☀ Note students' struggles and strategies as they attempt to even out the different shares.

Materials Needed

Field trip posters (or Appendix A)

Connecting cubes—one bin per pair of students

Calculators—one per pair of students

Scissors—one pair per pair of students

Large chart paper—a few sheets per pair of students

Markers

Developing the Context

☀ Display the field trip posters and summarize what students have discovered thus far.

☀ Ask students to investigate how much of a sub each person would have received if the seventeen subs had been shared equally among all twenty-two people.

Display the four field trip posters again and remind students of what is known so far:

1. Three subs for 4 people is $\frac{1}{2} + \frac{1}{4}$, or $\frac{3}{4}$, so 4 people each got $\frac{3}{4}$ of a sub

2. Four subs for 5 people is $\frac{1}{2} + \frac{1}{5} + \frac{1}{10}$, or $\frac{4}{5}$, so 5 people each got $\frac{4}{5}$ of a sub

3. Seven subs for 8 people is $\frac{1}{2} + \frac{1}{4} + \frac{1}{8}$, or $\frac{7}{8}$, so 8 people each got $\frac{7}{8}$ of a sub

4. Three subs for 5 people is $\frac{1}{2} + \frac{1}{10}$, or $\frac{3}{5}$, so 5 people each got $\frac{3}{5}$ of a sub

This distribution wasn't fair, and although it was a little fairer when two groups shared, it still wasn't fair. Now ask, "If the 17 subs had been shared by the 22 children fairly, about how much of a sub would each child have received?" Emphasize how it would not be practical to cut a sub up into 22 little pieces. Ask, "Is the amount about $\frac{1}{2}$, or $\frac{3}{4}$, or $\frac{2}{3}$? Where could one cut be made that would be a nice approximation?"

Behind the Numbers

If some students immediately say $\frac{17}{22}$, having constructed the idea of fractions as fair-sharing division from the work of the first two days, acknowledge that you agree but explain that you are wondering *about* how much that would be. In a real situation, no one is going to cut up a sub into 22 pieces, and you are wondering *about* how much that amount is so that the fewest possible cuts could be made. To clarify, you might ask, "Is it close to $\frac{1}{2}$, or $\frac{1}{4}$, or $\frac{3}{4}$, or $\frac{2}{3}$? Or is it almost a whole sub? About where should the cut go?" The main focus here is on the development of reasonableness, of judging the magnitude of fractional amounts.

☀ Note students' struggles and strategies as they attempt to even out the different shares.

Supporting the Investigation

Assign math partners and give each pair of students some large chart paper. Have calculators and connecting cubes available so that students may use them if they wish. Confer with students as needed to support and challenge their investigation. Have students make posters of their strategies and solutions.

Take note of the various struggles and strategies you see as students attempt to even out the different shares, including:

✦ making drawings or redistributing extra pieces by using the unit fractioning strategy from Day Four:

Some students may take away $\frac{1}{10}$ from each child in group #2 and give it to each child in group #4 so that each child in the combined group gets $\frac{1}{2}$ plus $\frac{1}{5}$. Next, they might remove the $\frac{1}{8}$ pieces from each of the kids in group #3, so that the children in groups #3 and #1 each receive $\frac{3}{4}$ of a sub. Redistributing the $\frac{7}{8}$ removed from group #3 to the ten children in groups #2 and #4 is difficult, but just encourage students to estimate. Estimation and magnitude in comparison to landmark fractions are the focus. Help students to realize that everyone gets approximately $\frac{3}{4}$ of a sub. [See Figure 7]

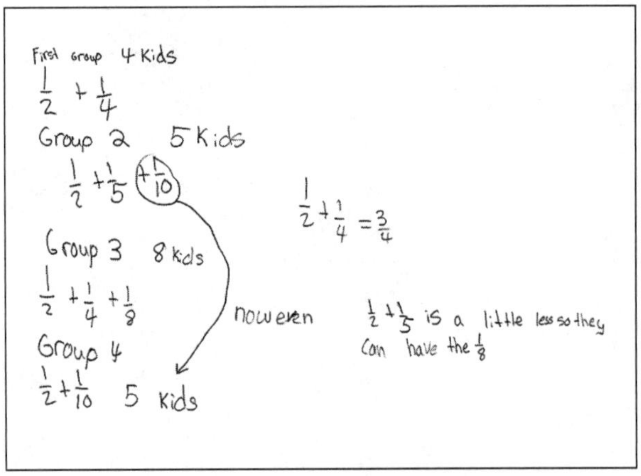

Figure 7

◆ cutting each sub into the same number of pieces as the number of children:

Some students may just divide each sub into 22 pieces and know that each child will get $17 \times \frac{1}{22}$, or $\frac{17}{22}$ of a sub. Now they will need to approximate what this amount is. Encourage them to think about what $\frac{1}{2}$ would be: $\frac{11}{22}$. Half of that to get a fourth is $\frac{5\frac{1}{2}}{22}$. Adding the half and fourth results in $\frac{16\frac{1}{2}}{22}$, which is $\frac{3}{4}$ and pretty close to $\frac{17}{22}$! So $\frac{17}{22}$ is about $\frac{3}{4}$. [See Figure 8]

◆ using the long division algorithm or a calculator to derive a decimal quotient:

17 divided by 22 is approximately 0.77. Since 0.75 is $\frac{3}{4}$, everyone should have received approximately $\frac{3}{4}$ of a sub.

◆ trying to build the subs with cubes:

Encourage students to consider what numbers might be helpful to use for a common-length sub, such as 40, and build it with connecting cubes. In this case the children in group #1 each get 30 out of 40 cubes; the children in group #2 each get 32 out of 40 cubes; the children in group #3 each get 35 out of 40 cubes; and those in group #4 each get 24 out of 40. Evening these amounts out results in about 30 out of 40 with 20 extra cubes to be distributed to 22 children, so an estimation would be $\frac{3}{4}$ of a sub, or $\frac{30}{40}$.

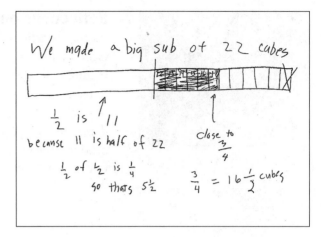

Figure 8

Behind the Numbers

As with the two-group redistributing problem, this investigation cannot be solved by averaging the fractions. The fractions cannot just be added up and divided by four because there are four groups. It is a weighted average situation—the subs need to be redistributed to the number of people, not the number of groups.

▥ Assessment Tips

As you move around and confer, take note of whether students seem to realize that with unit fractions, the greater the denominator, the smaller the piece is. Which students seem to understand that fractions can be thought of as division? Can they estimate the magnitude of the fraction? Are they clear that they are not adding the pieces together, but evening them out (averaging)? Can they work with landmark fractions to envision approximations and reasonableness of answers?

Differentiating Instruction

Keep grounded in the context to help students realize the meaning of what they are doing. Encourage them to think about landmark fractions and to estimate. Have students draw lines on their drawings of the subs to indicate where they would cut the subs. Provide as much chart paper as needed and have students cut out their drawings of the subs so they can then cut off pieces and move them to make approximate equivalent amounts.

Reflections on the Day

As the investigation of the redistributing of the subs progressed, students examined ways to share the subs more fairly and they worked with landmark fractions to develop a sense of the relative magnitude of messier fractions. They were encouraged to approximate equivalence. When adding fractions, students often erroneously add the numerators and denominators. As on Day Four, students explored how this process does not produce the addition of the fractional pieces, but instead results in a fraction in between the two fractions.

Discussing Strategies

S tudents meet in groups of eight or nine to discuss their strategies and findings from Day Five. A math congress is then convened to focus specifically on approximation strategies and magnitude in comparison to landmark fractions.

Day Six Outline

Preparing for the Math Congress

☀ Have students meet in small groups to share their posters.

☀ Listen to some of their conversations for ideas and strategies that should be discussed in the math congress.

Facilitating the Math Congress

☀ Have students discuss their strategies, insights, and ideas with a focus on developing their understanding of various strategies for approximating equivalence.

Materials Needed

Students' posters from Day Five

Class set of connecting cubes

Writing assignment (Appendix B)—one per student

Large chart pad and easel

Markers

Preparing for the Math Congress

☀ Have students meet in small groups to share their posters

☀ Listen to some of their conversations for ideas and strategies that should be discussed in the math congress.

Have the students take out their posters from Day Five and then convene three or four small groups. Appoint one person in each group to facilitate and have the students discuss their strategies. As they share, walk around and listen in on some of the conversations. In particular, listen for important ideas that might be worth discussing further in the math congress, such as how to choose a good number for a common-length sub (common denominators), interesting ways to redistribute, or how they know that given two fractions, combining the groups represented by the numerators and combining the groups represented by the denominators produces not a sum, but a fraction in between.

■ Tips for Structuring the Math Congress

As you listen in on the small-group conversations, do you notice any confusion? Are students able to see the relationships among the strategies? The upcoming congress will provide a forum to help students build an understanding of equivalence and magnitude in comparison to landmark fractions. To accomplish this, look for different strategies, including:

◆ adding up the total number of subs (17) and dividing that by the total number of people (22). Students may derive an approximation of $\frac{3}{4}$ by using $\frac{11}{22}$ as $\frac{1}{2}$ and then taking $\frac{1}{2}$ of that: $\frac{5\frac{1}{2}}{22}$.

◆ using the long division algorithm or a calculator to derive a decimal quotient: 17 divided by 22 is approximately 0.77. Since 0.75 is $\frac{3}{4}$, everyone should have received approximately $\frac{3}{4}$ of a sub.

◆ searching for a common-length sub, such as 40, building it with cubes, and making equivalent fractions: $\frac{3}{4} = \frac{30}{40}$; $\frac{4}{5} = \frac{32}{40}$; $\frac{7}{8} = \frac{35}{40}$; and $\frac{3}{5} = \frac{24}{40}$. Then redistributing the cubes so everyone gets 30 with a tiny bit of extra.

In the congress you will want students to develop an understanding of a variety of strategies for approximating equivalence. The main focus should be on developing a sense of the magnitude of messy fractions in relation to landmarks—for example, finding what $\frac{1}{2}$ or $\frac{1}{4}$ would be and using these as landmarks for estimating.

Facilitating the Math Congress

☀ Have students discuss their strategies, insights, and ideas with a focus on developing their understanding of various strategies for approximating equivalence.

After sufficient small-group discussion time, convene the students in the meeting area to discuss a few of the strategies they used or important insights or ideas they had.

A Portion of the Math Congress

Author's Notes

Caroline (the teacher)**:** As I walked around listening to your conversations, I overheard discussions on several different strategies for how you estimated. I thought this might make for an interesting discussion. Carlos and Maria, would you start us off by sharing your strategy?

Caroline frames the discussion so it is clear what the focus will be.

Maria: We made a sub that was 40 cubes long.

Caroline: Why 40?

Carlos: Actually we tried a lot of numbers first, but then we realized that 40 would be easier because we could divide it by 4, 5, and 8.

Caroline: Turn to the person next to you and discuss why Carlos and Maria chose 40. It seems they are proposing a way to compare the fractions. What do you think about their idea? *(Allows time for pair talk.)* Nadia?

Reasoning is examined, not just answers.

Pair talk encourages all the children to reflect on Maria and Carlos's strategy and to consider common denominators.

Nadia: It works. But you can do it with other numbers, too. We just used 17 divided by 22.

Sean: Yeah, but their strategy is different. And 40 is a good number for them.

Students are encouraged to examine each other's strategies, to understand, and to question.

Nadia: Why? I don't get it.

Carlos: Because then we could look at $\frac{3}{4}$ as $\frac{30}{40}$. (Maria holds up a stack of 40 cubes.) See, here (group #1) everybody got 30 out of 40. And here (group #2) everyone got 32, and here (group #3) they got the most, 35, and here (group #4) everyone got 24. Then we just evened the amounts out. If we give everybody 30 there is a little bit left over but not enough to give everyone another cube.

The students are encouraged to defend and justify their thinking.

Caroline: Carlos said a lot there! First let's see if everyone agrees that 30 of the 40 equals $\frac{3}{4}$. Melissa?

By slowing the conversation and encouraging the students to examine what has been said, Caroline ensures that everyone can participate in a conversation on equivalence.

Melissa: Well, $\frac{1}{2}$ is 20. And $\frac{1}{2}$ of that is 10.

Caroline: Nadia, I think you used $\frac{1}{2}$, and $\frac{1}{2}$ of $\frac{1}{2}$, too. Didn't you?

Caroline draws Nadia back into the conversation and in so doing establishes several equivalent relations, all in comparison to $\frac{3}{4}$.

Nadia: Yes. We started with the $\frac{17}{22}$. Michael and I made $\frac{11}{22}$ for $\frac{1}{2}$. We did $\frac{1}{2}$ of that and got $\frac{5\frac{1}{2}}{22}$.

Caroline: So let me write all of this up for us to look at: Carlos and Maria are saying that everyone got $\frac{30}{40}$ plus a little bit more. Melissa says that is $\frac{20}{40} + \frac{10}{40}$ plus a little more, or $\frac{1}{2} + \frac{1}{4}$, plus a little more. And Nadia, you say that you and Michael got $\frac{17}{22}$ exactly, and that was a little more than $\frac{11}{22}$, plus $\frac{5\frac{1}{2}}{22}$. Talk to the person next to you about this.

The expressions are written for examination and reflection. Caroline continues to focus students on equivalence, estimation, and comparison to landmark fractions, in this case $\frac{1}{2}$, $\frac{1}{4}$, and $\frac{3}{4}$.

■ Assessment Tips

After the math congress, jot down on sticky notes the big ideas you heard individual students express clearly and the strategies they used. Place these on the students' work along with any other anecdotal notes and put in students' portfolios. You may also want to photocopy the landscape of learning graphic (page 11) and, for each student, shade in the landmarks as you find evidence in their work. Note the students for whom you have no evidence. Over the next few days you will want to make special note of their work.

Hand out a copy of the writing assignment (Appendix B) to each student. Explain that they need to write about how they know that $\frac{1}{2} + \frac{2}{3}$ is not equal to $\frac{3}{5}$. This assignment can also be used as an individual assessment and placed in student portfolios.

Reflections on the Day

Students discussed redistributing strategies to establish a fairer situation and to estimate the magnitude of messy fractions like $\frac{17}{22}$ in relation to landmark fractions. Emphasis was placed on being able to estimate and judge comparatively by using landmark fractions—not on establishing exact equivalents. That will be the focus on Day Seven.

DAY SEVEN
Developing Equivalence

I n today's minilesson, students explore fractions as operators, for example as ½ of 24, and continue to examine equivalence. A new investigation then begins, developing a ratio table—a chart for fair sharing. The purpose of this investigation is to encourage the development of strategies to find equivalent fractions.

Day Seven Outline

Minilesson: A String of Related Problems

☀ Work on a string of related problems focused on fractions as operators.

☀ Represent students' strategies using chips on an overhead projector.

Developing the Context

☀ Display Appendix C and explain to students that you will use the chart to keep track of the number of subs needed for future field trips.

☀ Ask students to figure out how many subs would be needed for 4 people if each person gets about ¾ of a sub and record their answer on the chart.

Supporting the Investigation

☀ Support students as they work to complete the chart in Appendix C.

Preparing for the Math Congress

☀ Have students meet in small groups to share their strategies.

☀ Listen to some of their conversations for ideas and strategies that should be discussed in the math congress.

Facilitating the Math Congress

☀ Focus the math congress on generalizing strategies that can be used to find equivalent fractions.

Materials Needed

24 plastic chips

Student recording sheet for constructing a ratio table (Appendix C)—one per pair of students

Before class, prepare an overhead transparency of Appendix C.

Overhead projector, overhead markers and blank transparencies

Connecting cubes—one bin per pair of students

Scissors—one pair per student

Large chart pad and easel

Markers

Minilesson: A String of Related Problems (10–15 minutes)

* Work on a string of related problems focused on fractions as operators.

* Represent students' strategies using chips on an overhead projector.

Place 24 chips in a 4 by 6 array on an overhead projector and project onto a screen. Explore the following problems one at a time. Encourage various ways of determining the answers and establishing equivalence.

String of related problems:

$\frac{1}{2}$ **of 24**

$\frac{1}{4}$ **of 24**

$\frac{1}{8}$ **of 24**

$\frac{1}{3}$ **of 24**

$\frac{1}{4}$ **of 12**

$\frac{1}{2}$ **of 6**

Behind the Numbers

The focus of this string is making use of factors. The problems in the string are all related in that factors of 24 are used. The second problem can be solved by halving the answer of the first, the third by using the answer of the second. The third and fourth problems are also related. Doubling and halving is employed in the last two problems. Students will have a variety of ways to solve the problems in the string, however, and the relationships they offer should be explored and discussed.

Inside One Classroom

A Portion of the Minilesson

Caroline (the teacher): Here is an array, 4 by 6. I have 24 chips. What is $\frac{1}{2}$ of 24 and how do you know? Thumbs-up when you are ready. *(After noticing several thumbs.)* Lidia?

Lidia: Twelve. I made it a 4 by 3.

Caroline: Ok. Like this? You cut it in half this way? *(Draws a rectangle on the overhead around a 4 × 3 array, splitting the 4 × 6 array in half, vertically.)* Does everyone agree? Did anyone think of it a different way? Juan?

Juan: I did it as a 2 by 6.

Caroline: Like this? You cut it in half this way? *(Draws a rectangle around a 2 × 6 array, splitting the 4 × 6 array horizontally.)* OK if I write this: $\frac{1}{2}$ of 24 = 2 × 6 = 4 × 3? So how about this next one: $\frac{1}{4}$ of 24? Thumbs-up when you have an answer.

Paula: I did $\frac{1}{2}$ of the last problem— $\frac{1}{2}$ of $\frac{1}{2}$ is $\frac{1}{4}$, so 2 × 3.

Jeannie: Or $\frac{1}{4}$ of each column. That's one row. That's 6, too.

Author's Notes

Caroline provides think time and establishes a signal of thumbs-up when ready.

By recording the student's strategy, Caroline provides visual representation for comparison to other strategies as the string of related problems continues.

Alternative representations are recorded, and equivalence is established. As the string continues, all equivalent expressions are recorded and examined.

Developing the Context

Place the transparency of Appendix C on the overhead projector and project it onto a screen. Tell the students that you want to ensure that you won't ever make the same mistake as the teacher in the field trip story so you thought it might be a good idea to make a chart to keep track of the number of subs needed for future field trips. Tell them you think it is a good idea for everyone to get about ¾ of a sub. Ask them if they know how many subs that would be for 4 people. Encourage pair talk and then discuss in the whole group. Remind students that 3 subs for 4 people was ¾. Because this is the reverse of that scenario, the students may not see the connection immediately. Write in 3 (above the 4) on the chart. Pass out the recording sheets (Appendix C) and ask students to work in pairs to fill them out.

☀ Display Appendix C and explain to students that you will use the chart to keep track of the number of subs needed for future field trips.

☀ Ask students to figure out how many subs would be needed for 4 people if each person gets about ¾ of a sub and record their answer on the chart.

Supporting the Investigation

Have bins of connecting cubes available so that students may use them if they wish. You might also want to have extra chart paper available in case any students need to draw and then cut the pictures of the subs to be sure of the answers. As students work, confer with them as needed to support and challenge their investigation. Challenge strategies to become inquiries and encourage students to generalize.

This context introduces the ratio table as well as strategies for making equivalent fractions. Students might construct the ratio table in several ways:

☀ Support students as they work to complete the chart in Appendix C.

✦ Keeping the rate constant: if you double the number of people, you have to double the number of subs; if you triple the number of people, you have to triple the number of subs, etc.

✦ Using equivalent rates to make other equivalent rates: by combining the groups that are represented by the numerators and the denominators, 3 subs for 4 people and 6 subs for 8 people can be used to figure out 9 subs for 12 people.

✦ Repeated addition of the ¾.

▩ Assessment Tips

As you walk around supporting students, note the strategies they're using to determine equivalence. Which students need to cut up the subs to be sure the amount is still the same per person? Which keep the rate constant by using multiplication by 1 (as ²⁄₂ or ³⁄₃, etc.)? Which use partial quotients? It is helpful to jot down your observations on sticky notes. Later, you can place these notes on students' recording sheets to be included in their portfolios.

Preparing for the Math Congress

* Have students meet in small groups to share their strategies.

* Listen to some of their conversations for ideas and strategies that should be discussed in the math congress.

As you did on Day Six, convene three or four small groups. Appoint one student in each group to facilitate and have the students discuss their strategies. As they share, listen to some of the conversations for important ideas that might be worth discussing in the math congress. Help facilitate small-group discussion when needed to help students learn how to question each other. Ensure that discussions are helping others in the group to understand.

Facilitating the Math Congress

* Focus the math congress on generalizing strategies that can be used to find equivalent fractions.

After sufficient small-group discussion time, convene the students in the meeting area to discuss strategies that can be used to find equivalent fractions. The difference in this whole-group discussion vs. the small-group discussion is that now you will want to push for generalization of strategies for equivalent fractions.

Inside One Classroom

A Portion of the Math Congress

Caroline (the teacher): I noticed many wonderful strategies being used as I walked around and listened in to your discussions. Let's use our whole-group discussion today to make a list of the strategies, and let's try to justify why they work. Josi, you were talking about how you figured some out by adding subs and adding people. Would you explain that to us?

Josi: Well, we figured out that if there are 3 subs for 4 people, and 6 subs for 8 people, then $3 + 6 = 9$, and $4 + 8 = 12$, so 9 subs for 12 people is also fair.

Caroline: Hmmm… I saw a lot of you doing that. What's happening here? Why does that work? Are we adding fractions? $\frac{1}{2} + \frac{1}{4}$ doesn't equal $\frac{2}{6}$, does it? Talk to the person next to you about this. *(After pair talk.)* Jolanda?

Jolanda: $\frac{1}{2} + \frac{1}{4}$ can't be $\frac{2}{6}$ because $\frac{2}{6}$ is $\frac{1}{3}$. And besides, $\frac{1}{2} + \frac{1}{4}$ is $\frac{3}{4}$. *(Several murmurs of agreement.)*

Caroline: So what's going on with Josi's strategy then? It worked there, for the subs, right? Debbie?

Debbie: Josi is not adding fractions. She is making fair sharing. It's like the evening out we did the other day, when we added up all the subs and all the people, and we got $\frac{17}{22}$.

continued on next page

Author's Notes

Caroline frames the conversation right at the start by emphasizing the importance of generalizing and justifying.

By explicitly asking the students to consider if this ratio tabling strategy is about addition of fractions, Caroline encourages the students to reflect on what is happening, that it is not addition of the fractions. She thus prevents a common misconception from ever arising.

continued from previous page

Michael: Oh, I get it. It's like evening out two things that are already even, because ¾ and ⁶⁄₈ are already equal, so if you add the subs and then add the people you just get another situation that is equal.

Caroline: What if we wanted to know how many subs for 5 people?

Simone: Then it is 3 and ¾ subs. One more person, ¾ of a sub for them.

Caroline: OK. What other strategies or things did you notice?

Simone: When you double the subs, you have to double the people.

Jolanda: ⁹⁄₁₂ is triple. Well not really triple. It is equal, but 12 is triple 4, and 9 is triple 3.

Caroline: Hmmm… Does this mean that whatever we do to one we have to do to the other to keep it fair? Can we generalize this?

By using a simple case of just one more person, five instead of four, students have a chance to consider why the addition of subs and kids keeps the shares equivalent.

Students are encouraged to invent and share what they notice and then pushed to generalize.

Reflections on the Day

Today students continued to explore equivalent relations. They were introduced to the ratio table and developed several strategies that could be used to make equivalent fractions.

DAY EIGHT
The Fund-Raiser

Materials Needed

Bike course poster
[If you do not have the full-color poster (available from Heinemann), you can use the smaller black-and-white version in Appendix D.]

Sixty-inch tape measures—one per pair of students

Large chart paper—one sheet per pair of students

Large chart pad and easel

Markers

The day begins with a mental math minilesson on division, designed to encourage a strategy of making equivalent values that are easier to work with—for example, simplifying $\frac{300}{12}$ to $\frac{100}{4}$. A new context—the design of a bike course for a charity fund-raiser—is then developed to support the emergence of the bar, or double number line, model. Students record points on a 60k course for markers of sixths, thirds, quarters, halves, tenths, fifths, eighths, and twelfths. The representation is then used to explore equivalent fractions.

Day Eight Outline

Minilesson: A Division String

☀ Work on a string of related problems designed to support simplifying as a strategy for whole-number division.

☀ Record students' strategies on an open array.

Developing the Context

☀ Display the bike course poster and tell students they will be designing their own bike course.

Supporting the Investigation

☀ Support and confer with the students as they work on their bike course posters, noting the variety of strategies being used.

Minilesson: A Division String (10–15 minutes)

This mental math minilesson uses a string of related problems to encourage students to explore how it is sometimes easier to simplify first when dividing. As before, do one problem at a time. This time, record the students' strategies on the open array. If you notice students beginning to make use of equivalent problems as you progress through the string, discuss why this strategy is helpful. If the class agrees that it is a useful strategy, you might want to make a sign for it and post it near the meeting area. Over time you will have several signs of "Helpful Division Strategies" posted around the room.

☀ Work on a string of related problems designed to support simplifying as a strategy for whole-number division.

☀ Record students' strategies on an open array.

String of related problems:

100/4

200/4

200/8

400/16

300/12

600/24

Behind the Numbers

The string has been crafted to support simplifying as a strategy for whole-number division. The quotient of the second problem is twice the amount of the quotient in the first because the dividend is twice the amount, while the divisor stays the same. In the third problem, the divisor doubles. The quotient is thus half of the quotient in the second problem, but now equivalent to the quotient of the first. Relationships like this occur throughout the string. Support students to discuss the relationships they notice and to explore what happens to the quotients. Use the open array to represent their strategies.

Inside One Classroom

A Portion of the Minilesson

Caroline (the teacher)**:** So let's start today with $^{100}/_4$. Show me with your thumbs when you are ready. Sally?

Sally: It's 25. I just thought of it as quarters, money.

Caroline: I bet a lot of you did. Yes? OK. Let's just go on to the next one. How about $^{200}/_4$?

Billie: It's twice as much.

Caroline: Let me draw an array. Here's the first problem:

```
          25
      ┌─────────┐
   4  │   100   │
      └─────────┘
```

Author's Notes

Caroline knows that most of the students have a good sense of four quarters in a dollar so she does not spend much time here, but moves on to the harder problems in the string.

The open array is drawn as a model that can be varied and used as a tool to explore the relationships among the problems as the string continues.

continued on next page

continued from previous page

So now we have twice as much inside, but still four rows. Let's see what that array would look like:

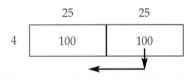

What about this one: $200/8$? Turn to the person next to you and talk about this one. Also talk about what you think the array will look like.

Pair talk is used for think time and reflection. Students are also encouraged to imagine how the array will change.

Josh: I know the answer is half of the last answer. I'm not sure about the array.

Maria: I think it just moves down.

Caroline: What moves down?

Maria: The last array, the 100. It moves down and over.

Caroline: Like this? *(Draws an array with an arrow.)*

As the remainder of the string is done, the arrays will be used to investigate the relationships among the problems. Equivalence among some of the problems will also be established—for example, 200/8 = 100/4.

Developing the Context

☀ Display the bike course poster and tell students they will be designing their own bike course.

Display the bike course poster (or Appendix D) and explain that students will be designing a course for a two-day-long, 60k bike trip—a charity fund-raiser. Since this is a two-day event, hotels are needed at the halfway point to allow everyone to rest well in the evening. Explain that the following landmarks should also be indicated on the course:

✦ Resting points at every eighth of the course

✦ Food wagons at every fourth of the course

✦ Water stations at every tenth of the course

✦ Juice and snack tables at every fifth of the course

✦ Kilometer markers placed along the course so bikers can calculate how much of the course they've completed. People who have pledged money will be paying for every kilometer biked. These markers should be placed at every twelfth, sixth, and third of the course, as well as at all the other locations listed above. These markers should indicate how many kilometers have been completed.

Supporting the Investigation

Distribute sixty-inch measuring tapes to each pair of students. Have the pairs draw a sixty-inch bike course on large chart paper. As the students work, move around to support and confer as needed. A variety of strategies are likely to be used, including the following:

☀ Support and confer with the students as they work on their bike course posters, noting the variety of strategies being used.

+ halving: using landmark fractions and taking a half—for example, finding fourths by halving the half or finding eighths by halving fourths

+ dividing by the denominator—for example, $\frac{1}{4}$ of 60 = $\frac{60}{4}$

+ adding pieces—for example, $\frac{3}{8}$ is $\frac{1}{8}$ more than $\frac{2}{8}$

+ using equivalence strategies developed with the ratio table from Day Seven, such as constant rate—for example, $\frac{6}{8}$ is equivalent to $\frac{3}{4}$, because 6 is twice 3, and 8 is twice 4

■ Assessment Tips

Note the strategies that students are using. Note the growth and development students are making on the landscape of learning graphic. Remember to pay particular attention to the students for whom you do not have evidence.

Differentiating Instruction

For students who are struggling, stay in the context. Have them fold the measuring tape to find the marks and discuss with them how many portions are being made. For students who may need more of a challenge, have them calculate the fractional parts of each kilometer (such as halves, fourths, and eighths of an inch, as on the tape measure), mark them on their plans, and then calculate the fractional part of the course. For example, $\frac{1}{2}$ of an inch (if an inch represents one kilometer) is $\frac{1}{120}$ of the course.

Reflections on the Day

Students' understanding of equivalence was further developed today as they focused on simplifying as a strategy for whole-number division. Today's context, designing a bike course, supported the development of the measurement model for fractions. This is in contrast to the fair-sharing model of the first week. Students determined fractional markers along the bike course by using the strategies developed with the ratio table. They discovered that several markers would be common points and that these common points are equivalent fractions, which can be marked on a bar or a number line. This model can be extended to include a double number line as a helpful model for addition and subtraction of fractions. For more on how this model can be used for operations with rational numbers, see the *Contexts for Learning Mathematics* resource unit *Minilessons for Operations with Fractions, Decimals, and Percents.*

DAY NINE

The Fund-Raiser

Materials Needed

Students' posters from Day Eight

Sixty-inch tape measures —one per pair of students

Sticky notes—one pad per student

Large chart pad and easel

Markers

The day begins with a mental math minilesson on division, designed once again to encourage a strategy of making equivalent values that are easier to work with. Students then return to work to finish designing the bike course, but today they are asked to specifically focus on three questions:

1. What locations have multiple landmarks?
2. What do they notice about the relationships of the markers?
3. What strategies did they use (and find most helpful) to determine the locations?

A congress is then held to discuss these questions and a chart is made of all the equivalent fractions.

Day Nine Outline

Minilesson: A Division String

* Work on a string of related problems designed to support simplifying as a strategy for whole-number division.
* Record students' strategies on an open array.

Preparing for the Math Congress

* Have students review their bike course posters and answer some additional questions.
* Conduct a gallery walk for students to review and post comments on each other's posters.
* Listen to students' conversations and determine who should share during the math congress.

Facilitating the Math Congress

* As students report their findings, record the list of locations that had multiple markers.
* Discuss the patterns and relationships that students notice.

Minilesson: A Division String (10–15 minutes)

As on Day Eight, this mental math minilesson uses a string of related problems to encourage students to simplify first when dividing. As before, do one problem at a time. Record the students' strategies on an open array.

☀ Work on a string of related problems designed to support simplifying as a strategy for whole-number division.

☀ Record students' strategies on an open array.

String of related problems:

60/4

120/4

240/8

480/16

960/32

240/16

2400/160

Preparing for the Math Congress

Working with their partners from Day Eight, have students answer these three questions:

1. What locations have multiple landmarks?

2. What do you notice about the relationships of the markers?

3. What strategies did you use (and find most helpful) to determine the locations?

Students should include their responses on the posters they created on Day Eight.

Once students have had sufficient time to investigate these questions, lay their posters out on tables or display them around the room and have a gallery walk. Ask students to review all the posters and see if they agree with where everyone has placed the markers. Students should record their questions and/or comments on sticky notes and place them on the posters. As students review and discuss each other's work, listen for important ideas regarding equivalent fractions that might be worth discussing in the whole group. As needed, facilitate small-group discussion to help students learn how to question each other and how to read and make comments.

▦ Tips for Structuring the Math Congress

In the math congress you will be posting a list of equivalent fractions (where multiple landmarks are) and establishing ways to be sure they are equivalent. You will also be discussing relationships, such as the fact that the fifths occur at every other tenth. Keep equivalence in mind as you observe the gallery walk so that you can decide which students' ideas should be the focus of the discussion.

Behind the Numbers

As students progress through the string, encourage them to think about how the arrays are related. For example, $\frac{120}{4}$ is equivalent to $\frac{240}{8}$ in that the quotient—the length—stays the same. In other words, the area and the number of rows change, but proportionally. Students may be confused that the arrays are not equivalent and it is important to emphasize that the length is.

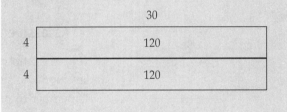

☀ Have students review their bike course posters and answer some additional questions.

☀ Conduct a gallery walk for students to review and post comments on each other's posters.

☀ Listen to students' conversations and determine who should share during the math congress.

Facilitating the Math Congress

☀ As students report their findings, record the list of locations that had multiple markers.

☀ Discuss the patterns and relationships that students notice.

After sufficient time for the gallery walk, convene the students in the meeting area to discuss the three questions. As students report a list of all locations that had multiple markers (question #1), record them on large chart paper. For example:

$$\tfrac{1}{2} \ = \ \tfrac{2}{4} \ = \ \tfrac{4}{8} \ = \ \tfrac{5}{10} \ = \ \tfrac{3}{6} \ = \ \tfrac{6}{12} \ = \ \tfrac{30}{60}$$

| Hotel | Food | Rest | Water | km marker | km marker | km marker |

Once all of the equivalent fractions are up on a chart, shift the discussion to the patterns and relationships that the students noticed (question #2). Some students may have noticed that once all the twelfths were placed for the km markers, the sixths and thirds were already done. Discuss why that happened. Encourage students to notice that 12 is a multiple of 3 and of 6. Examine where else the twelfths landed (for example, the food wagons) and ask if 12 is a multiple of those numbers, too.

Other students may have noticed that the juice and snack tables were at every other water station and that the food wagons were at every other resting point. Encourage students to examine why this pattern occurred: how are fifths and tenths related? how are fourths and eighths related?

■ Assessment Tips

Note the strategies that students are using. Also note the growth and development students are making on the landscape of learning graphic. Remember to pay particular attention to the students for whom you do not have evidence.

Reflections on the Day

A measurement model was discussed today as students continued to explore equivalent fractions. They noticed how multiples were helpful—for example, how twelfths, sixths, and thirds are related, and halves, fourths, and eighths are related. The minilesson focused on equivalent relations as well, encouraging students to simplify when possible for whole-number division.

Fraction Bar Capture

The unit culminates today with the introduction of Fraction Bar Capture, a game students can play even after the unit is completed. The game makes use of fraction bars, which students try to capture by finding equivalent relations.

Day Ten Outline

Developing the Context

☀ Model how to play Fraction Bar Capture.

Supporting the Investigation

☀ Support and challenge students to consider more difficult captures and note the strategies they use to prove equivalence.

Materials Needed

Fraction Bar Capture game cards (Appendix E)—one deck per pair of students

Instructions for making fraction bars (Appendix F)—four copies per pair of students

Student recording sheet for Fraction Bar Capture (Appendix G)—one per pair of students

Markers

Scissors—one pair per student

Developing the Context

☀ Model how to play Fraction Bar Capture

Bring the students to a meeting area and have them sit in a circle. Play Fraction Bar Capture with one student as a way to introduce the game to the class and model how the game is played.

■ Object of the Game

This game is designed to provide students with experiences in building equivalent relations with fractions. The objective is to capture all the fraction bars. Players work cooperatively toward this goal.

■ Directions for Playing Fraction Bar Capture

Students play the game in pairs. Each pair of students must first create 30 fraction bars, as described in Appendix F. The fraction bars are then spread out on the table faceup. The game cards (Appendix E) are stacked facedown. Players take turns turning over a card. An equivalent amount of fraction bars is captured and removed from the table. For example, if the card says $\frac{6}{8}$, players could capture $\frac{1}{2}$ and $\frac{1}{4}$ (since this amount is equivalent to $\frac{6}{8}$) or they could capture $\frac{9}{12}$ or $\frac{3}{4}$ or $\frac{6}{8}$. They must determine the relation they want to capture as they cannot capture all of them, only one equivalent relation. The capture is recorded on the recording sheet (Appendix G). For example, $\frac{6}{8} = \frac{9}{12}$ would be recorded if the $\frac{9}{12}$ fraction bar was captured. Players work together to capture all the bars until none are left on the table.

Supporting the Investigation

☀ Support and challenge students to consider more difficult captures and note the strategies they use to prove equivalence.

Students are assigned math partners and go to tables to play the game. Each pair of students has a set of fraction bars, a recording sheet, and a stack of cards. Move around and confer with students as they play the game. Support and challenge them to consider more difficult captures and to prove they are equivalent—for example, using $\frac{5}{6}$ to capture $\frac{1}{2}$ and $\frac{1}{3}$.

■ Assessment Tips

Note the strategies that students are developing for proving equivalence. Now that the unit is coming to a close, review the work in students' portfolios and your anecdotal notes. Look at each learner's pathway as you shade in the landmarks on the landscape of learning graphic. Where are they on the landscape of learning for fractions? Document their progress. Make a note of what landmarks are ahead.

Make a class display—a sociohistorical wall—documenting the progression of the unit, the important ideas constructed over the past two weeks, samples of students' posters, and a description of some of their strategies for making equivalent fractions. By making this display available you allow your students to revisit and reflect on all the wonderful ideas and strategies they constructed throughout the unit.

Reflections on the Unit

The mathematician Reuben Hersh said, "It's the questions that drive mathematics. Solving problems and making up new ones is the essence of mathematical life. If mathematics is conceived apart from mathematical life, of course it seems—dead" (1997, page 18). When mathematics is understood as mathematizing one's world—interpreting, organizing, inquiring about, and constructing meaning through a mathematical lens—it becomes creative and alive.

Traditionally mathematics has been taught in our schools as if it were a dead language. It was something that mathematicians had created in the past—something that needed to be learned, practiced, and applied. When the definition of mathematics shifts toward the activity of mathematizing one's lived world, the constructive nature of the discipline and its connection to problem solving become clear.

In this unit, students were invited to find ways to mathematize situations in their own lived worlds. They explored fair sharing of sub sandwiches and developed a chart for field trips to ensure fair sharing in the future. They formulated various strategies for making equivalent fractions, and they designed a bike course for a fund-raiser. Within all of these rich contexts they were developing several big ideas, strategies, and important models for rational numbers. They also worked hard on strategies for efficient computation for division and explored how fractions are related to division.

Name _____ Date _____

■ Write a convincing argument for the following statement:

$$\tfrac{1}{2} + \tfrac{1}{3} \text{ does not equal } \tfrac{2}{5}$$

Names _____ Date _____

■ Chart for class-size groups:

Subs										
People	1	2		4	5			8		10

Subs										
People		12				16				20

Subs										
People				24	25			28		

■ Chart for larger groups:

Subs										
People				48			60			120

■ The cafeteria workers don't want to make a chart for every size group. Are there any general rules they could use that would be helpful?

■ Design a 60k bike course. Add sign markers for the following:

☐ Resting points at every $\frac{1}{8}$th of the course

☐ Food wagons at every $\frac{1}{4}$th of the course

☐ Water stations at every $\frac{1}{10}$th of the course

☐ Juice and snack tables at every $\frac{1}{5}$th of the course

☐ Km signs at every $\frac{1}{12}$th of the course indicating how many km have been completed

☐ Km signs at every $\frac{1}{6}$th of the course indicating how many km have been completed

☐ Km signs at every $\frac{1}{3}$rd of the course indicating how many km have been completed

60K Bike Course Fund-raiser

- You can make these cards more durable by pasting them on oaktag and laminating them.

$\frac{1}{2}$	$\frac{1}{3}$	$\frac{1}{4}$	$\frac{1}{12}$
$\frac{1}{6}$	$\frac{2}{3}$	$\frac{2}{4}$	$\frac{2}{12}$
$\frac{2}{6}$	$\frac{3}{12}$	$\frac{2}{6}$	$\frac{3}{3}$

$\frac{3}{6}$	$\frac{4}{6}$	$\frac{3}{12}$	$\frac{4}{12}$
$\frac{6}{12}$	$\frac{3}{4}$	$\frac{8}{12}$	$\frac{9}{12}$
$\frac{12}{12}$	$\frac{2}{3}$	$\frac{10}{12}$	$\frac{5}{6}$
$\frac{2}{4}$	$\frac{6}{8}$	$\frac{5}{12}$	$\frac{7}{12}$

■ Make copies and cut out the strips below. Make 30 fraction bars shading in the following: $\frac{1}{2}$, $\frac{1}{4}$, $\frac{3}{4}$, $\frac{1}{3}$, $\frac{2}{3}$, $\frac{1}{6}$, $\frac{1}{12}$, $\frac{2}{12}$, $\frac{3}{12}$, $\frac{4}{12}$, $\frac{5}{12}$, $\frac{9}{12}$, $\frac{2}{6}$, $\frac{2}{8}$, $\frac{8}{12}$. Make two of each.

Names _____ Date _____

Card   What I captured

_____ = _____

_____ = _____

_____ = _____

_____ = _____

_____ = _____

_____ = _____

_____ = _____

_____ = _____

_____ = _____

_____ = _____